PYRAMIDS OF GIZA

Sheelagh Matthews

www.av2books.com

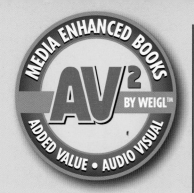

AV² provides enriched content that supplements and complements this book. Weigl's AV² books strive to create inspired learning and engage young minds in a total learning experience.

Your AV² Media Enhanced books come alive with...

Audio
Listen to sections of the book read aloud.

Key Words
Study vocabulary, and complete a matching word activity.

Video
Watch informative video clips.

Quizzes
Test your knowledge.

Embedded Weblinks
Gain additional information for research.

Slide Show
View images and captions, and prepare a presentation.

Try This!
Complete activities and hands-on experiments.

... and much, much more!

Go to www.av2books.com, and enter this book's unique code.

BOOK CODE

G 9 1 5 6 5 9

AV² by Weigl brings you media enhanced books that support active learning.

Published by AV² by Weigl
350 5th Avenue, 59th Floor
New York, NY 10118
Website: www.av2books.com   www.weigl.com

Library of Congress Cataloging-in-Publication Data

Matthews, Sheelagh.
 Pyramids of Giza / Sheelagh Matthews.
    p. cm. -- (Virtual field trips)
 ISBN 978-1-61690-767-9 (hardcover : alk. paper) -- ISBN 978-1-61690-771-6 (paperback : alk. paper) --
ISBN 978-1-61690-435-7 (online)
1. Pyramids of Giza (Egypt)--Juvenile literature. 2. Pyramids of Giza (Egypt)--Design and construction--
Juvenile literature. I. Title.
 DT63.K576 2011
 932--dc23
                    2011019314

Printed in the United States of America in North Mankato, Minnesota
1 2 3 4 5 6 7 8 9 0 15 14 13 12 11

052011
WEP290411

Editor: Heather Kissock
Design: Terry Paulhus

Every reasonable effort has been made to trace ownership and to obtain permission to reprint copyright material. The publishers would be pleased to have any errors or omissions brought to their attention so that they may be corrected in subsequent printings.

Weigl acknowledges Getty Images as its primary image supplier for this title.

Contents

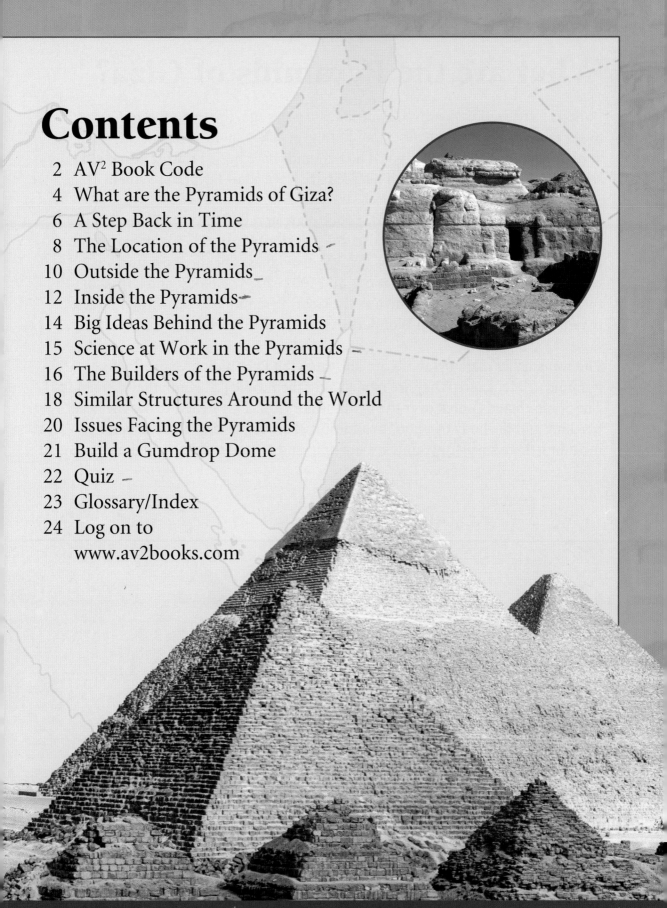

What are the Pyramids of Giza?

Built by a civilization that lived almost 4,500 years ago, the Pyramids of Giza tower majestically over the desert land of Egypt. They stand as one of the best-known symbols of Ancient Egypt. The pyramids have been a tourist attraction since they were built. Millions of people have traveled to Egypt to see them.

The pyramids are located on a strong rock **plateau** called the Giza Plateau, a few miles (kilometers) south of Cairo, the capital of Egypt. They consist of three pyramid complexes built as tombs for Egyptian kings. The three pyramids at Giza were built over three generations and 100 years. The oldest and largest of the three main pyramids is known as the Great Pyramid. It is the world's largest pyramid and the only **Seven Wonders of the Ancient World** that remains today.

The two smaller main pyramids are known as the Pyramid of Khafre and the Pyramid of Menkaure. They are named after the people for whom they were built. The Sphinx stands watch over the Pyramids of Giza. This structure has the head of a king and the body of a lion. In addition, there are several other structures, including three smaller pyramids, a boat pit, and several temples and **mastabas**.

The Pyramids of Giza are an imposing sight on the Egyptian desert.

Snapshot of Egypt

Egypt is located mainly in northeast Africa. A small piece of the country called the Sinai Peninsula extends into southwest Asia. Egypt is bordered by the Mediterranean Sea to the north, Sudan to the south, and Libya to the west. The Red Sea makes up most of Egypt's eastern border. However, the Sinai Peninsula shares a border with Israel and the Gaza Strip.

INTRODUCING EGYPT

CAPITAL CITY: Cairo

FLAG:

POPULATION: 82,079,636 (2011)

OFFICIAL LANGUAGE: Arabic

CURRENCY: Egyptian pound

CLIMATE: A desert climate, with hot, dry summers and moderate winters

SUMMER TEMPERATURE: 86° to 95° Fahrenheit (30° to 35° Celsius)

WINTER TEMPERATURE: 68° to 79° F (20° to 26° C)

TIME ZONE: EET (Eastern European Time)

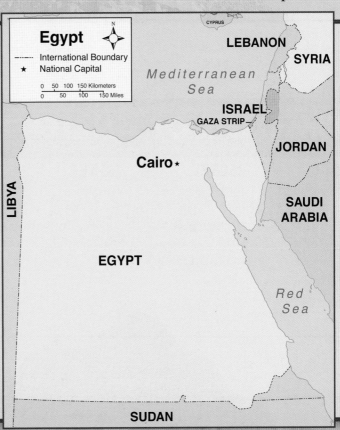

Arabic Words to Know

When visiting a foreign country, it is always a good idea to know some words and phrases of the local language. Practice these phrases to prepare for a trip to Egypt.

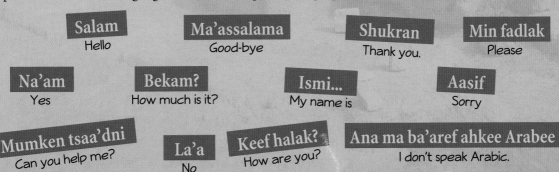

Salam
Hello

Ma'assalama
Good-bye

Shukran
Thank you.

Min fadlak
Please

Na'am
Yes

Bekam?
How much is it?

Ismi...
My name is

Aasif
Sorry

Mumken tsaa'dni
Can you help me?

La'a
No

Keef halak?
How are you?

Ana ma ba'aref ahkee Arabee
I don't speak Arabic.

A Step Back in Time

Egypt is a very old civilization. Its history is divided into several periods, generally following the rule of 30 **dynasties**. A dynasty is a series of rulers from the same royal family. The greatest of these periods are the Old Kingdom (2700–2200 BC), Middle Kingdom (2050–1800 BC), and New Kingdom (1550–1070 BC). The Pyramid Age belongs to Egypt's Old Kingdom, but kings of the Old, Middle, and New Kingdoms were all buried in pyramids.

TIMELINE OF ANCIENT EGYPT

5000 BC
People begin to settle the area, using the fertile land in the Nile Valley for farming.

3500 BC
Egyptians begin using **hieroglyphic** writing to record information.

2630 BC
The first pyramid, the Step Pyramid of Djoser, is built.

2613 BC
Sneferu becomes king and begins building three small pyramids near the Step Pyramid of Djoser.

2575–2150 BC
The Pyramids of Giza are built for King Khufu, his son King Khafre, and his grandson, King Menkaure.

Khafre ruled from 2520 to 2494 BC. He built the second-largest pyramid at Giza.

The Step Pyramid of Djoser is located at Saqqarah, about 15 miles (24 kilometers) southwest of present-day Cairo.

As pyramids took a long time to build, the first duty of an Egyptian king was to start construction of his tomb. The tomb would house a king's body in the **afterlife**. Bodies of kings were preserved as **mummies** and placed in their pyramids after death. Ancient pyramids contained priceless jewelry, beautiful sculptures, and walls of hieroglyphic engravings and paintings.

Each mummy was placed in an ornate container called a sarcophagus. The sarcophagus of King Tutankhamen is one of the best known. He ruled Egypt from 1333–1323 BC.

2000–1900 BC
The first **obelisk** is built.

1539–1075 BC
Royal tombs are built in the Valley of the Kings. King Tutankhamen rules for a short period.

969 BC
The city of Cairo is founded.

51–30 BC
Queen Cleopatra reigns over Egypt.

30 BC
Egypt becomes a province of the **Roman Empire**.

For almost 500 years, Egypt's kings and their families were buried in the Valley of the Kings.

Due to its age, Cairo's architecture is an interesting blend of old and new.

The Location of the Pyramids

Ancient Egyptians believed that, after death, their kings went to live with the gods in the Kingdom of Osiris. Osiris was the god of the Underworld. It was believed that a pyramid, a structure that pointed toward the heavens, could help a king's spirit rise to the kingdom. Pyramids were aligned with the stars in **Orion's constellation**, as these stars were believed to house the soul of Osiris.

Accuracy in measuring and positioning was extremely important in pyramid building. The sides of the Great Pyramid are oriented to the four compass points—north, south, east, and west. Astronomers helped with the orientation by aligning the Great Pyramid with the stars. Then, surveyors measured and leveled the site. If the alignment of the sides was wrong, they would not meet at the top.

The site where the pyramids sit is called the Giza Necropolis. A necropolis is a large burial site. Besides kings, the Giza Necropolis was a burial site for wealthy nobles and commoners.

The Pyramids Today

The Giza Plateau is located on the west bank of the Nile River and is bordered by the city of Giza and the Sahara Desert. There were many advantages to choosing the Giza Plateau to construct the pyramids. As these monuments are extremely heavy, they need a strong base, or foundation, underneath them. The hard stone plateau provides a surface strong enough to withstand the enormous weight of the pyramids. The plateau is also high enough to keep the pyramids above the water during the Nile River's annual flood.

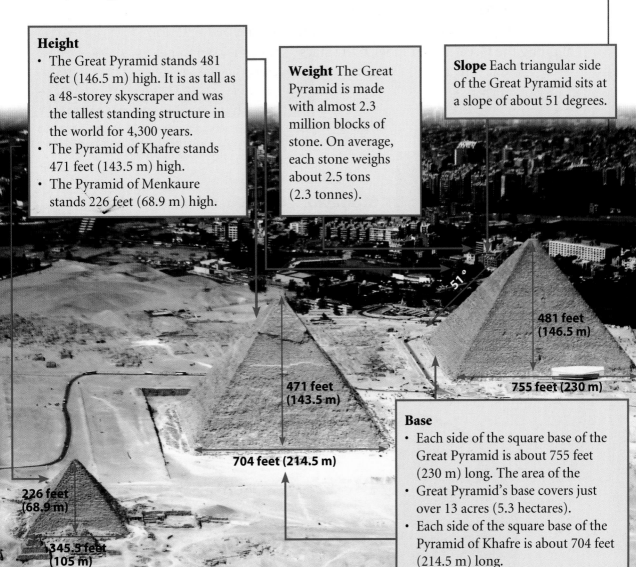

Height
- The Great Pyramid stands 481 feet (146.5 m) high. It is as tall as a 48-storey skyscraper and was the tallest standing structure in the world for 4,300 years.
- The Pyramid of Khafre stands 471 feet (143.5 m) high.
- The Pyramid of Menkaure stands 226 feet (68.9 m) high.

Weight The Great Pyramid is made with almost 2.3 million blocks of stone. On average, each stone weighs about 2.5 tons (2.3 tonnes).

Slope Each triangular side of the Great Pyramid sits at a slope of about 51 degrees.

481 feet (146.5 m)

51°

471 feet (143.5 m)

755 feet (230 m)

704 feet (214.5 m)

226 feet (68.9 m)

345.5 feet (105 m)

Base
- Each side of the square base of the Great Pyramid is about 755 feet (230 m) long. The area of the
- Great Pyramid's base covers just over 13 acres (5.3 hectares).
- Each side of the square base of the Pyramid of Khafre is about 704 feet (214.5 m) long.
- Each side of the square base of the Pyramid of Menkaure is about 345.5 feet (105 m) long.

Outside the Pyramids

Rising up over the city of Giza, their solid rock exteriors are just one of the many features the pyramids possess.

Stone Exterior The pyramids are made mostly of limestone and granite. The granite forms the inside layer, with a casing of polished limestone lying overtop. At one time, the polished limestone reflected sunlight to such a degree that the pyramid could be seen for miles.

At one time, the Great Pyramid had more than 100,000 casing stones. These stones were removed approximately 600 years ago to build other structures.

Each block on the pyramids is separated by less than 0.02 inches (.51 millimeters). The blocks are held in place by a form of cement.

Stonework The cornerstones of the pyramids have balls and sockets built into them. This means that the stones are rounded and fit inside a cavity inside another stone. Ball and socket joints help the pyramid manage the expansion and contraction movements caused by heat and cold.

The Great Pyramid does not have a capstone. Some believe that the pyramid never had one.

Capstone The **capstone** is the triangular stone that sits on top of the pyramid, forming its point. Capstones were usually made of stone but often had a gold casing. This made them shine brightly in the Sun.

Other Structures Each of the three pyramids has a **causeway** that connects the pyramid to a temple in the Nile River valley. Boat pits at the base of the Great Pyramid and the Pyramid of Khafre are believed to have been storage places for the kings' boats. Boat pits have not been found at the Pyramid of Menkaure.

In 1954, the funerary boat for King Khufu was discovered. It has since been reconstructed and is on display in a building near Khafre's pyramid.

Surrounding Buildings Two of the pyramids have subsidiary buildings near them. The Great Pyramid has three smaller pyramids and three groupings of mastabas. The Pyramid of Menkaure has two mastabas and one small pyramid near its base.

The remains of a mortuary temple have been found near the Pyramid of Khafre.

Door A hinged door covers the Great Pyramid's entrance, which is about 59 feet (18 m) above the pyramid's base. When closed, the door is barely noticeable from the outside.

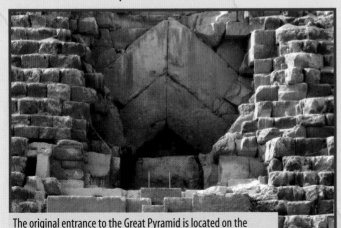

The original entrance to the Great Pyramid is located on the pyramid's north face.

VIRTUAL TOUR

After an earthquake in the 14th century, the Pyramids of Giza were looted by robbers. Ancient treasures, such as paintings, sculptures, pottery, weapons, jewelry, and other personal belongings, were stolen.

Inside the Pyramids

To gain a full understanding of the pyramids, a tour inside is a must. Only then can the craftsmanship and planning of the builders be truly appreciated. A trip inside the Great Pyramid allows visitors to see the work that went into creating a pyramid.

Passages Upon entering the Great Pyramid, visitors begin walking down a hallway. After about 97 feet (29.6 m), the hallway separates into upward and downward passages. The downward passage leads to two underground chambers. The upward passage leads to the king's and the queen's chambers. For the most part, the passages are only about 3.5 feet (1 m) wide and 4 feet (1.2 m) tall. However, the upward passage opens up as visitors approach the chambers. This large hallway is called the Grand Gallery.

The Grand Gallery is 26 feet (8 m) high and 153 feet (46.6 m) long. The stone blocks that make up its walls angle inward. This is called corbelling.

The Queen's Chamber is notable for its lack of decoration. Its walls and ceiling are bare, and the room is devoid of contents. A recess in the wall is believed to have once housed a statue.

Queen's Chamber The Queen's Chamber is located at a lower level than the King's Chamber. The room is about 18 feet (5.5 m) by 17 feet (5.2 m) and has a height of 20 feet (6.1 m). The walls are made of granite. The Queen's Chamber never housed a queen. Queens were buried in pyramids of their own. As a result, the purpose of the room is unclear. It does not appear to have ever been used.

Air Shafts The Great Pyramid has four air shafts leading into the structure. Two shafts lead into the king's chamber. Two others lead into the queen's chamber. Only those connected to the king's chamber extend to the outside of the pyramid. There are several theories about the purpose of the shafts, but no definitive reason for their presence has been confirmed.

Of all the pyramids in Egypt, only the Great Pyramid of Khufu has air shafts.

Visitors can only travel upward toward the King's and Queen's chambers. The downward passage and underground chambers are closed to the public.

Underground Chambers There are two rooms in the underground section of the pyramid. The first room is the smaller of the two. The large room measures 46 by 27 feet (14 by 8 m) with a ceiling of 11 feet (3.3 m). The ceiling is smooth, but the floor of the room is rough. Some people call it the "upside down room" because of this. In the center of the floor is a deep pit. It is sometimes called the "bottomless pit" because no one knows how far it extends into the ground.

King's Chamber The King's Chamber is at the end of the Grand Gallery. It measures 34 by 17 feet (10.4 by 5.2 m) and has a height of 34 feet (10.4 m). The red-granite sarcophagus of the king sits inside the room. Five rooms are located just above the King's Chamber. The rooms were created to support the heavy stonework and ensure that the ceiling of the King's Chamber did not collapse under the weight.

Due to its size, archeologists believe that the sarcophagus was put in the room before the pyramid's construction was complete.

Big Ideas Behind the Pyramids

Building any structure requires planning, physical labor, and technology. The people who built the pyramids had to use their knowledge of scientific principles to ensure that the structures were strong and durable.

The Pyramids of Giza were constructed using equal-sized triangles, each supporting the other as they rose to a point at the top.

Geometry and Triangles

In ancient Egypt, basic **geometrical** figures were used to build the pyramids. The base of a pyramid, for instance, is a square. A pyramid's sides, however, are made of four equal triangular sides that meet in a point. Triangles are basic parts of geometry. They are the strongest and most stable shapes known to humans. Unlike a four-sided frame, a triangle shape will not collapse, or fail. For example, if force is applied to the corner of a square, the square becomes a diamond shape. If force is applied to the corner of a triangle, its shape stays the same.

Withstanding Weight

The Pyramids of Giza were built on the solid stone of the Giza Plateau. This high, flat, and hard area made an excellent construction site. It was able to support the heavy load of the pyramids. Loads are forces that act on structures, such as weight, wind, temperature, or vibration. The weight of any structure itself is called a "dead load." A soft surface, like the desert sand, would not have been strong enough to support the Pyramids of Giza. The pyramids would have experienced "settlement load" on a soft surface. This means they would have sunk and possibly changed shape if built on sand.

The Great Pyramid is one of the heaviest structures on Earth.

Science at Work in the Pyramids

The ancient Egyptians constructed the massive pyramids without the help of machines or power tools. However, they used innovative technology and hand tools to ease their workload.

Ramps are useful in today's world as well. They help people move objects from one level to another.

Ramps

Ramps are inclined planes. An inclined plane is a flat surface that is slanted. Inclined planes allow things to be moved with less effort. The ancient Egyptians did not have mechanical cranes to lift a pyramid's heavy stone blocks into place. Instead, they may have dragged the stone blocks up to the pyramid using ramps. Some historians believe that one long ramp was used. As the pyramid rose higher, the ramp became longer. This made sure the ramp was never too steep. Other historians believe that ramps went around the pyramid. Ramps were made using mud, stone, and wood.

Wedges

Stone-cutting tools were used to cut a pyramid's massive stone blocks from the **quarry**. Many of these tools were wedges. Wedges use the pointed end of an inclined plane to do work. A wedge pushes things apart by converting motion in one direction into a splitting motion at

A wedge is an object with at least one slanting side that ends in a sharp edge. The edge is used to cut material apart.

the other end. The splitting occurs at right angles to the pointed part of the wedge. The handheld wedges used to cut the stone for the pyramids were made out of a type of stone that was harder than the stone being quarried for the pyramid. This allowed the wedges to cut into the rock without breaking.

VIRTUAL TOUR

Before the first pyramid was built, tombs for kings were large structures, but much lower in height. They were mastabas constructed of mud brick, instead of stone.

The Builders of the Pyramids

Kings appointed their own royal architects to oversee the construction of their pyramid in ancient Egypt. The main architect of the Great Pyramid was Hemon, a relative of King Khufu. Hemon, however, would have been highly influenced by the work of an architect named Imhotep. Many other laborers also contributed to the construction of the pyramids.

Imhotep Pyramid Designer

Imhotep is considered to be the world's first architect. He is known as the designer of the first pyramid ever to be built, the Step Pyramid of Djoser, at Saqqarah, Egypt. The inventor of stone construction, Imhotep is thought of as the first structural engineer. The same methods he developed are used in the construction of structures today.

The entrance to King Djoser's tomb is a great hall lined with large stone columns. Building with stone was new to the Egyptians. It is possible that Imhotep designed and built the first architectural columns known to humankind.

Besides being an architect and engineer, Imhotep also wrote many works on medicine. He is considered to be one of the world's first physicians.

Hemon Chief Architect, Great Pyramid

Hemon is believed to have been a nephew to King Khufu. He was also known as Khufu's vizier, or chief advisor. King Khufu ordered that no expense be spared on building his tomb. It was to be a large and grand monument to him. The scope of the project added years to its construction. It took an estimated 20 years to build the pyramid. More than 20,000 workers are believed to have contributed to its construction.

Hemon is buried in a mastaba close the Great Pyramid. Several statues in his likeness have been found there.

King Khufu ruled from 2589 to 2566 BC. His mummy has never been found. The only likeness of him is a small statue that now resides in the Cairo Museum.

Stonemasons

Stonemasons were responsible for cutting the core blocks for the pyramids and shaping the stone. After the ramps were removed from the pyramids and the construction materials were cleared away, stonemasons began working on the surface of the structures. They would smooth and polish the rock to give it a refined finish. Today, masons continue to work on buildings. They shape bricks and stones and lay them in place.

Today, stonemasons help to restore old structures that have become damaged over time.

Laborers

Laborers made up the majority of workers on the Pyramids of Giza. Many laborers were farmers who built the pyramids when they were not working the land. Laborers were responsible for doing many tasks. They lifted heavy rocks, prepared meals, and carried water.

Laborers continue to play an important role in construction. They perform many jobs, including building concrete forms, loading materials, and operating equipment.

Carpenters

Carpenters played an important role in the construction of the pyramids. They made tools that were used by other trades. Carpenters carved wooden statues and adornments for the inside of the pyramids. These workers are important to construction today. They perform many different woodworking tasks. Some carpenters build the frames for buildings, such as houses. Other carpenters make furniture. Most carpenters learn the trade by working with others who are skilled at the craft.

Carpenters use a variety of woodworking tools, including chisels.

Similar Structures Around the World

Different types of pyramids are found all around the world. Other cultures built pyramids as temples or capitals of empires instead of tombs. Not all pyramids from other cultures are made of stone. Some are made of mud and brick, others with glass and steel. Today's modern architects use the pyramid form to construct office buildings, museums, and monuments. Small pyramids cap the tops of obelisks.

Etemenanki

BUILT: 625–539 BC
LOCATION: Babylon, ancient Mesopotamia
DESIGN: Sumerians
DESCRIPTION: Etemenanki was a seven-storey **ziggurat** that was dedicated to a god named Marduk. Today, little remains of the structure that likely inspired Biblical stories of the Tower of Babel.

The seven stories of Etemenanki reached a height of 299 feet (91 m).

Templo Mayor consisted of two stepped pyramids rising up from a single platform.

Templo Mayor

BUILT: Around 1390 AD
LOCATION: Mexico City, Mexico
DESIGN: Aztecs
DESCRIPTION: This stepped pyramid was built as a temple to two Aztec gods. Templo Mayor was mostly destroyed in 1521, when the Aztecs were conquered by Spain.

Canary Wharf Tower

BUILT: 1991
LOCATION: London, England
DESIGN: Cesar Pelli, architect
DESCRIPTION: At 800 feet (244 m) high, this 50-storey skyscraper is capped with a pyramid, making the structure look like a giant obelisk. It houses 6.6 million square feet (613,000 sq. m) of office space.

Canary Wharf tower is the second tallest building in the United Kingdom.

Transamerica Pyramid

BUILT: 1970
LOCATION: San Francisco, California
DESIGN: William L. Pereira & Associates, architects
DESCRIPTION: Transamerica Insurance & Investment Group built this landmark office building. It is 48 stories high, with 530,000 square feet (49,239 sq. m) of space. Its largest floor measures 145 feet (44 m) per side. Its smallest floor measures only 45 feet (14 m) per side.

The two "wings" on each side of the pyramid house a stairwell on one side and elevator shafts on the other.

Issues Facing the Pyramids

The physical environment can have a big effect on a structure. Built in the desert, the Pyramids of Giza have withstood several forces of nature, from winds and floods to earthquakes. Still, the pyramids are not in the same condition as they were when constructed. Time and the environment have brought their share of damage.

WHAT IS THE ISSUE?

Windstorms and sandstorms are common in the desert. The desert's hot sun and blowing sand has weathered the pyramids' stone blocks.

When people visit the site, they pollute the area by leaving garbage, such as pop cans and food wrappers, behind.

Humans have vandalized the pyramids and their surroundings by etching their names in the stone and taking pieces of the pyramids as souvenirs.

EFFECTS

The wind has stripped small particles of stone from the pyramids' walls. This is called erosion.

Litter makes the environment unsafe for visitors and ruins the beauty of the site.

The vandalism has damaged the integrity of the site and its building materials.

ACTION NEEDED

The Egyptian government closes one of the pyramids every year for restoration work. This work takes place on both the interior and exterior of the pyramid.

The Pyramids of Giza have been named a **UNESCO World Heritage Site**. UNESCO is providing technical assistance and training to preserve the site.

Security cameras, fencing, and motion detectors have been placed throughout the site to monitor people's actions around the pyramids.

Build a Gumdrop Dome

Triangles are the most stable building unit. One of the strongest building structures, made entirely of triangles, is known as a **geodesic dome**. Each triangle is connected to another one. These shapes form a rigid, but spherical framework, creating a dome. Each side of every triangle shares the load of the weight of this building equally.

Geodesic domes are strong, lightweight, and easy to construct. Try building a small-scale geodesic dome out of gumdrops and toothpicks.

Materials
- 11 gumdrops
- 25 toothpicks that are pointed at both ends

Instructions

1. Use gumdrops to connect five toothpicks in a ring. This will result in a base that is in the shape of a pentagon.

2. Use two toothpicks and one gumdrop to make a triangle on one side of this base.

3. Repeat, making triangles all around the pentagon-shaped base.

4. Use toothpicks to connect the gumdrops at the tops of the triangles. How many triangles do you have?

5. Push one toothpick into each of the top gumdrops.

6. Use the last gumdrop to connect these toothpicks at the top.

7. Try testing the dome's strength by pressing down on one point of its many triangles. What does it do?

8. Using extra gumdrops and toothpicks, make a box. Press down on one of the points of the box. What does it do? How does this compare to the triangle?

Pyramid Quiz

Q Who was responsible for the first pyramid ever built?

A King Djoser ordered the construction of the first pyramid. Imhotep was the architect.

Q What are the characteristics of a pyramid?

A A pyramid has four equal triangular sides that rise to a point. The base of a pyramid is square.

Q How was the Great Pyramid positioned on the landscape?

A Astronomers aligned the Great Pyramid with the stars in the night sky. Then, surveyors measured and leveled the site.

Q What are loads?

A Loads are forces, such as weight, wind, temperature, and vibrations, that act on structures.

Glossary

afterlife: the time after a person's death

capstone: the top stone on a structure

causeway: a raised road or path, as across low or wet ground

dynasties: families or groups that maintain power for several generations

geodesic dome: a light, structural framework arranged as a set of polygons in the form of a shell

geometrical: concerned with a branch of mathematics that deals with measurement

hieroglyphic: relating to an ancient Egyptian language using symbols for words and numbers

mastabas: flat-roofed, rectangular mud-brick buildings found above underground burial chambers; from the Arabic word for bench, as these structures have a similar shape to a bench

mummies: preserved bodies wrapped in strips of linen

obelisk: a tall square-shaped tower capped by the shape of a pyramid

Orion's constellation: a group of stars that form a specific design

plateau: flat and tablelike land, usually higher than the land around it

quarry: an open excavation or pit from which stone is obtained

Roman Empire: areas ruled by Roman emperors

Seven Wonders of the Ancient World: the seven structures considered by scholars to be the most wondrous of the ancient world

UNESCO World Heritage Site: a place designated by the United Nations Educational, Scientific and Cultural Organization to be of cultural significance to the world and in need of protection

ziggurat: a form of temple tower built in Mesopotamia, somewhat like a stepped pyramid with a flat top

Index

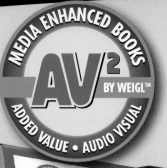

Log on to www.av2books.com

AV² by Weigl brings you media enhanced books that support active learning. Go to www.av2books.com, and enter the special code found on page 2 of this book. You will gain access to enriched and enhanced content that supplements and complements this book. Content includes video, audio, web links, quizzes, a slide show, and activities.

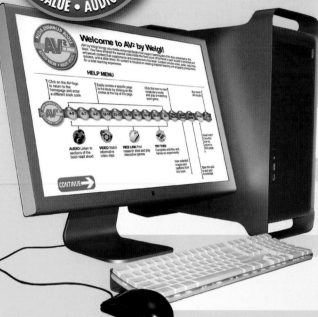

Audio
Listen to sections of the book read aloud.

Video
Watch informative video clips.

Embedded Weblinks
Gain additional information for research.

Try This!
Complete activities and hands-on experiments.

WHAT'S ONLINE?

Try This!	Embedded Weblinks	Video	EXTRA FEATURES
Test your knowledge of Arabic.	Find out more about where the pyramids are located.	Watch a video introduction to the pyramids.	
Test your knowledge of the history of the pyramids in a timeline activity.	Learn more about a notable person from the history of the pyramids.	Watch a video about another tour destination near the pyramids.	**Audio** Listen to sections of the book read aloud.
Learn more about the math behind the pyramids.	Learn more about becoming an architect.		**Key Words** Study vocabulary, and complete a matching word activity.
Compare modern architects with ancient ones.	Find out more about other important structures near the pyramids.		**Slide Show** View images and captions, and prepare a presentation.
Write about an issue in your community that is similar to one facing the pyramids.			**Quizzes** Test your knowledge.
Complete a fun, interactive activity about the pyramids.			

AV² was built to bridge the gap between print and digital. We encourage you to tell us what you like and what you want to see in the future.

Sign up to be an AV² Ambassador at www.av2books.com/ambassador.